Puzzles

Find your way through

Climb the ladders

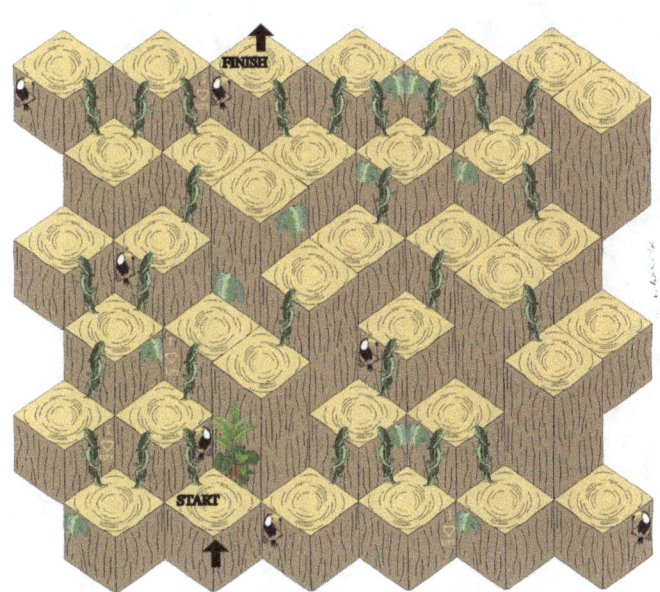

Climb the vines

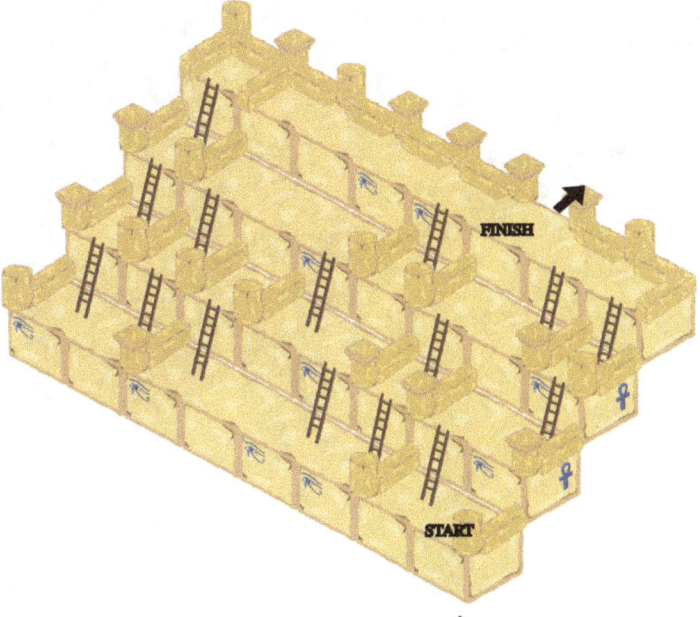

Get to the top of the stairs

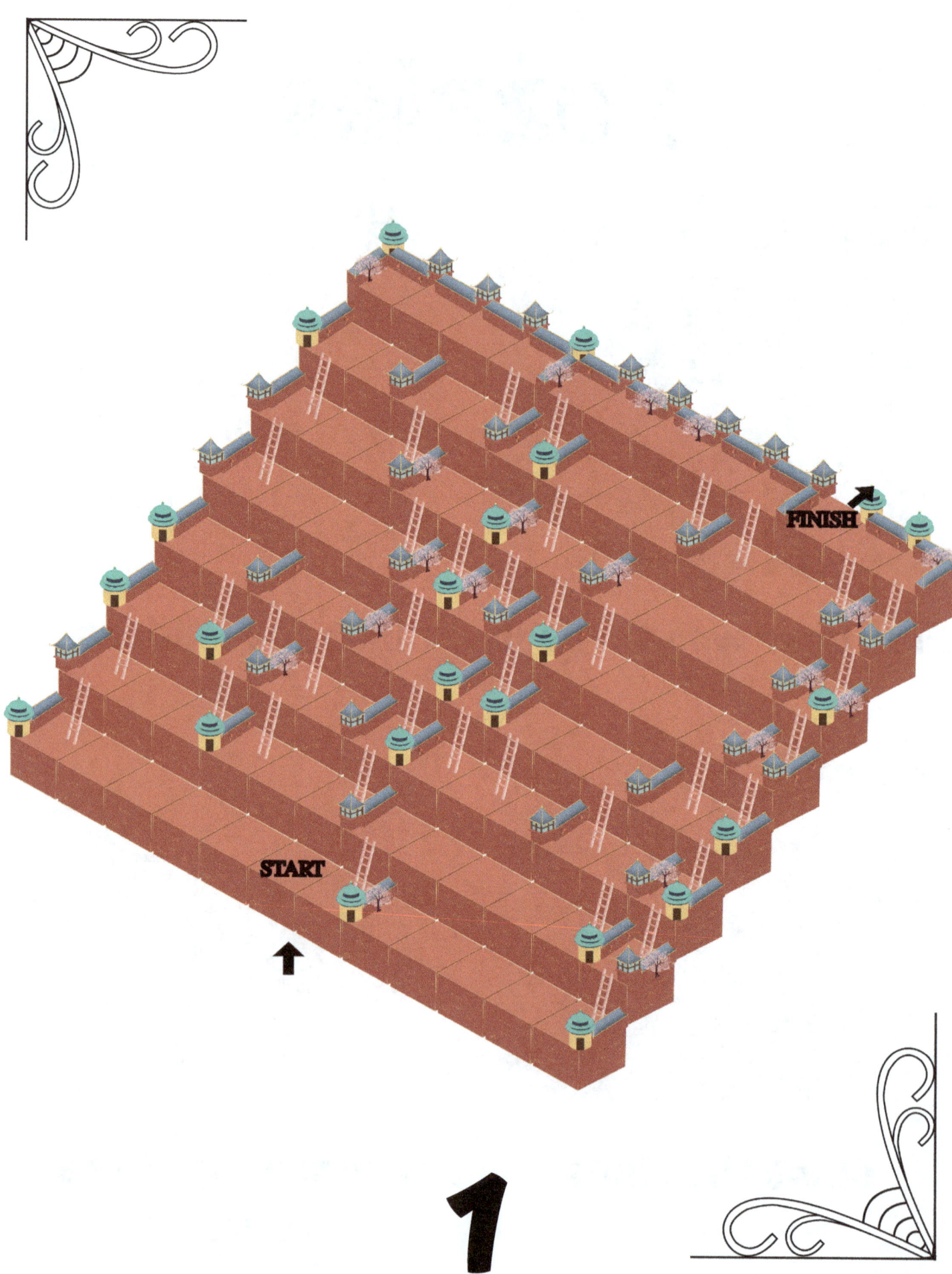

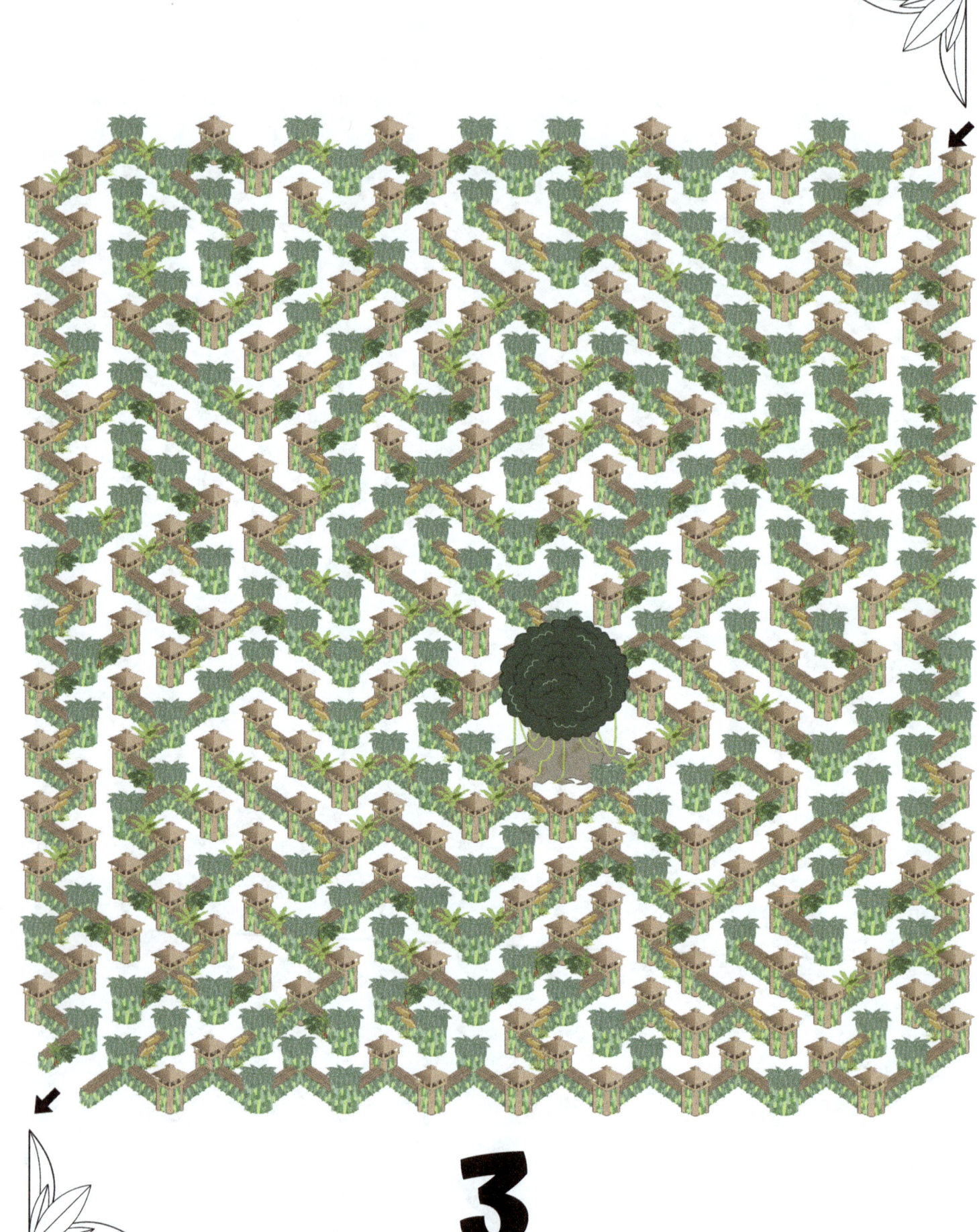

3

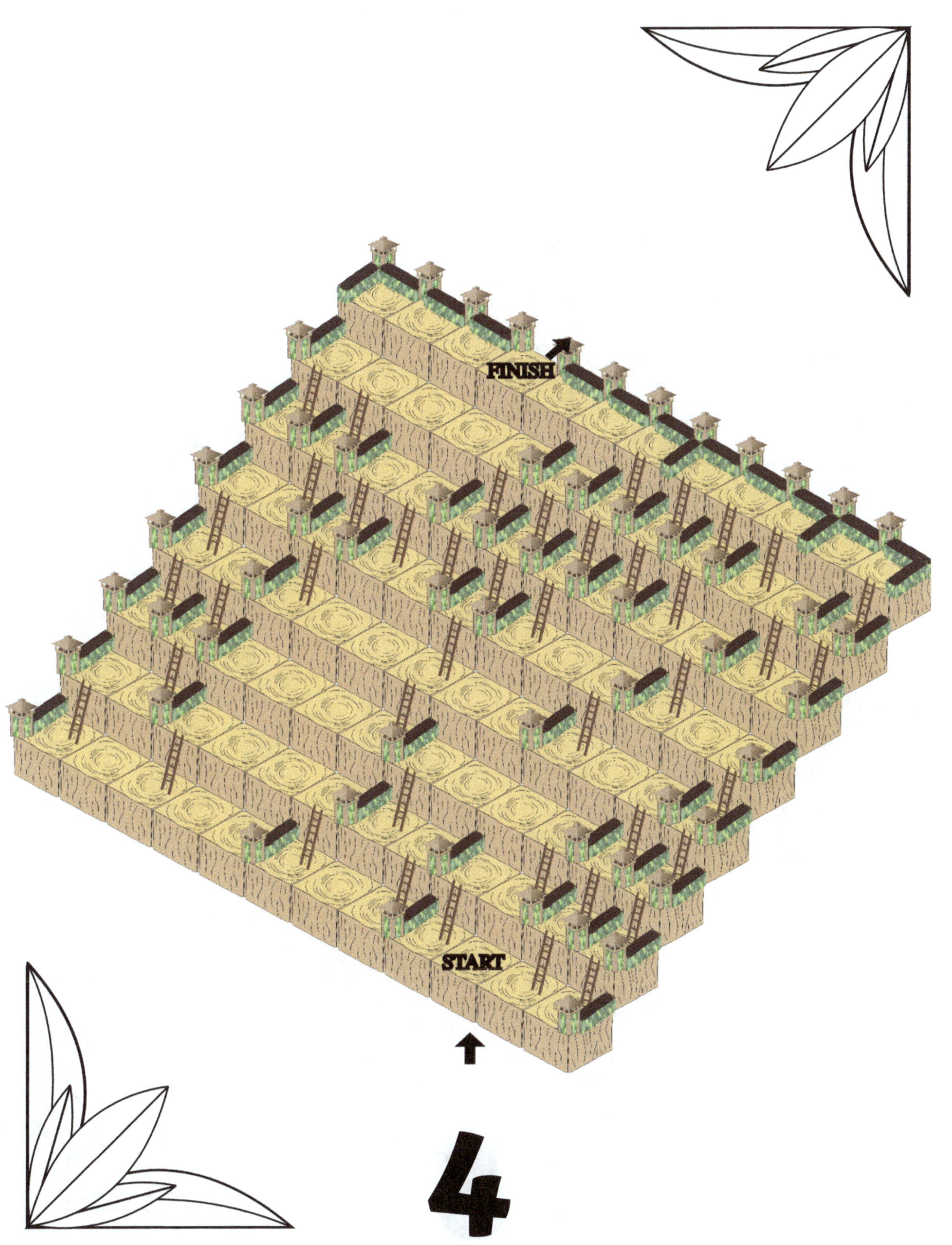

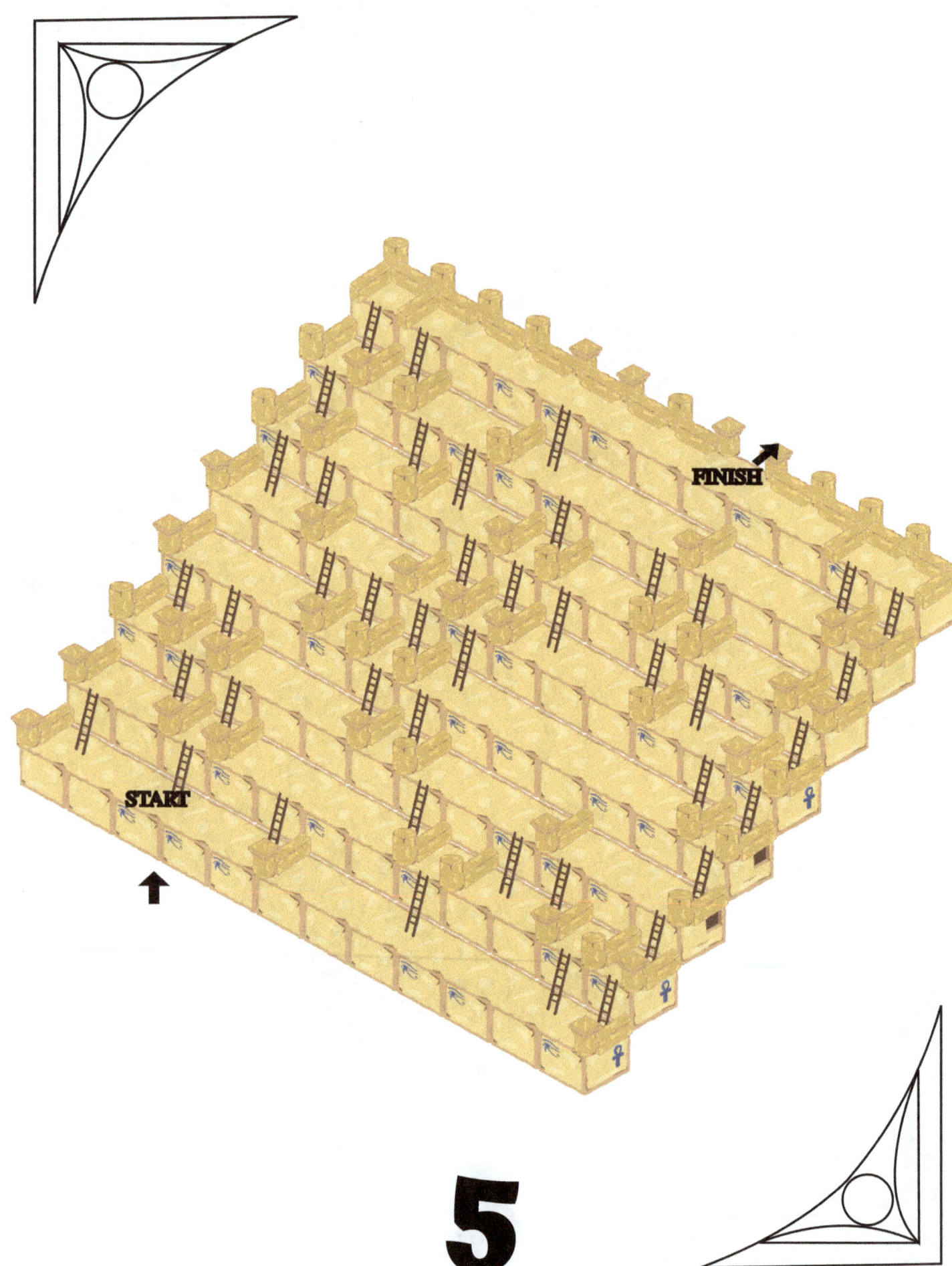

6

7

8

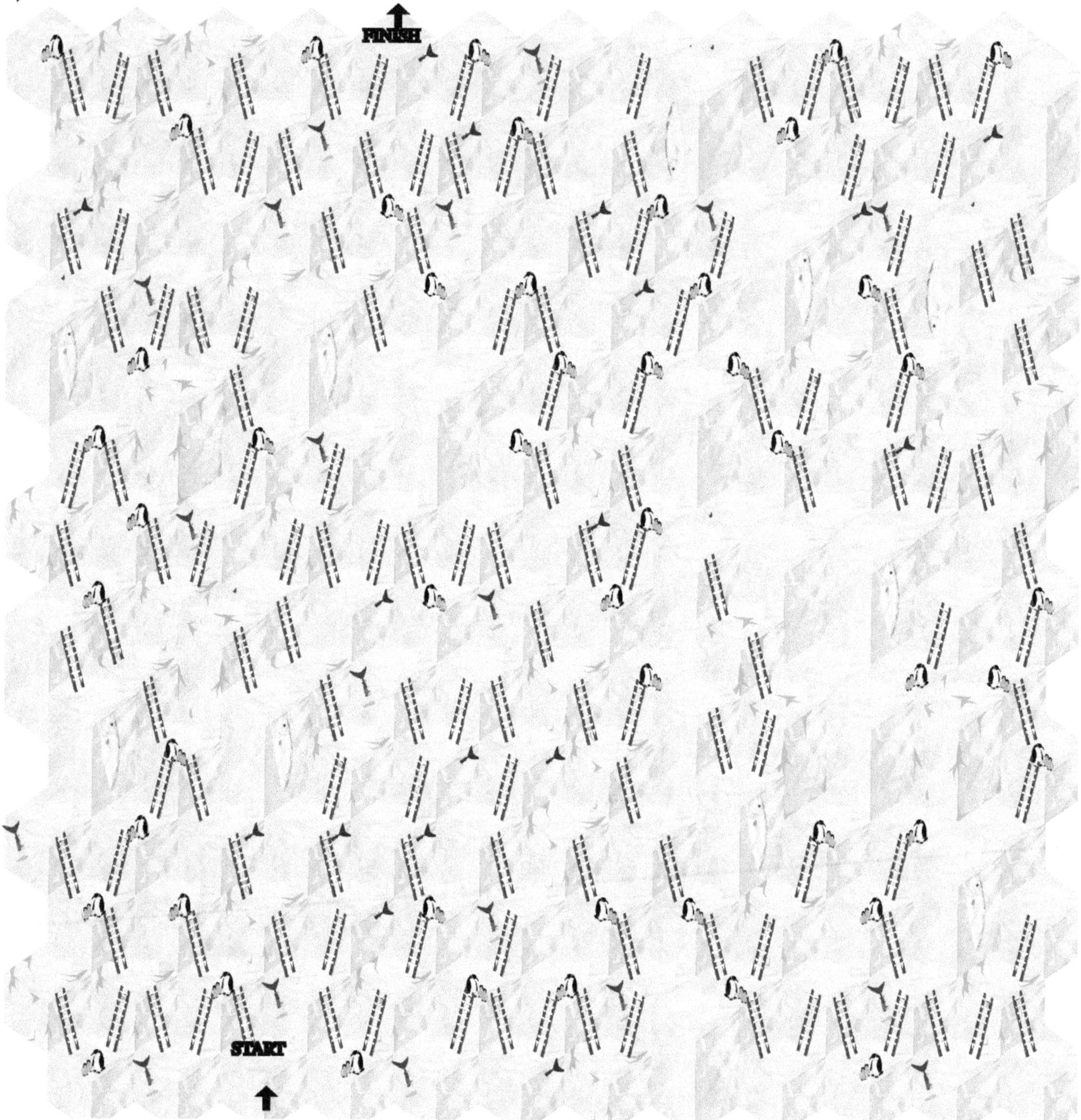

9

10

11

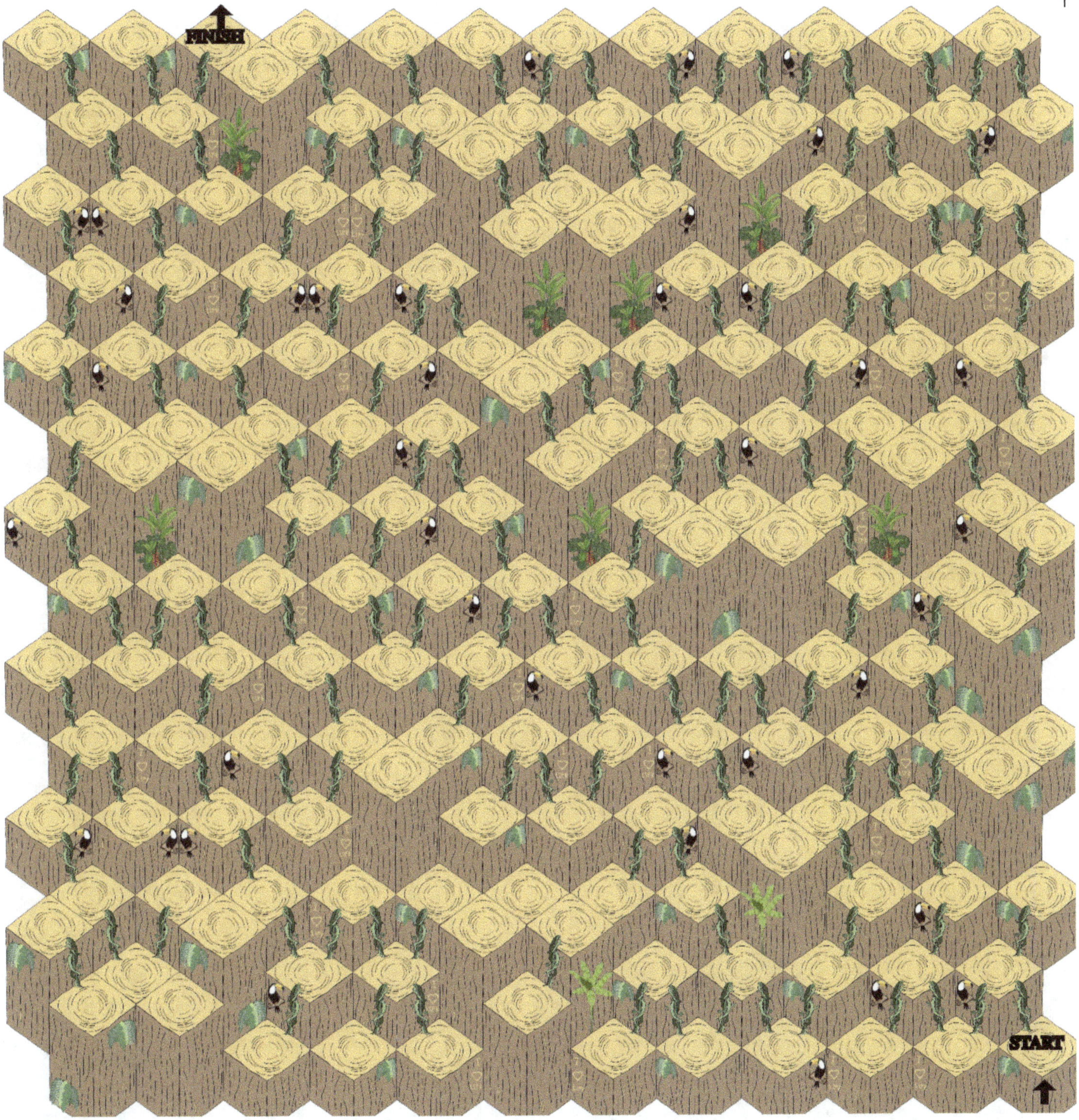

12

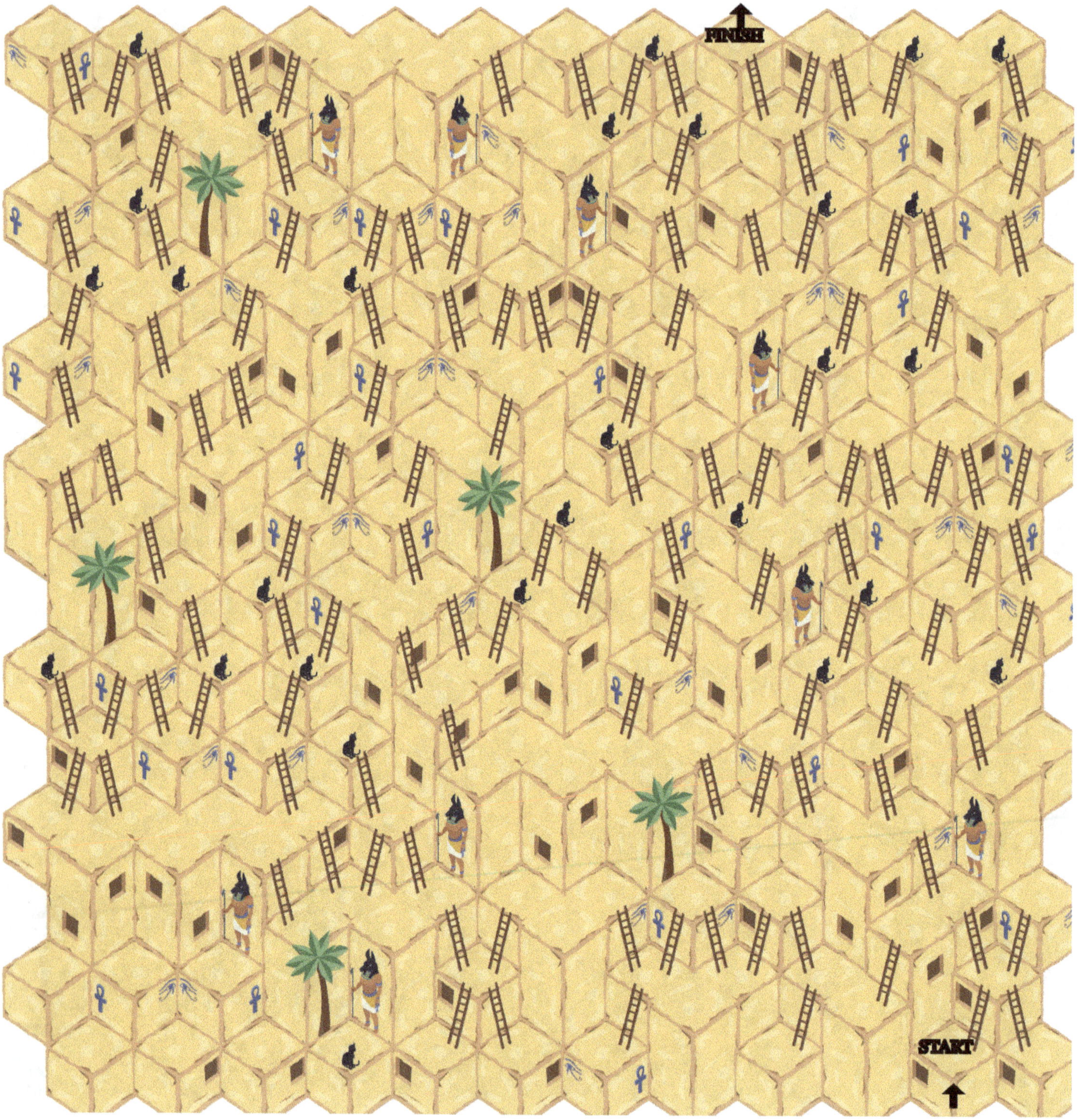

13

14

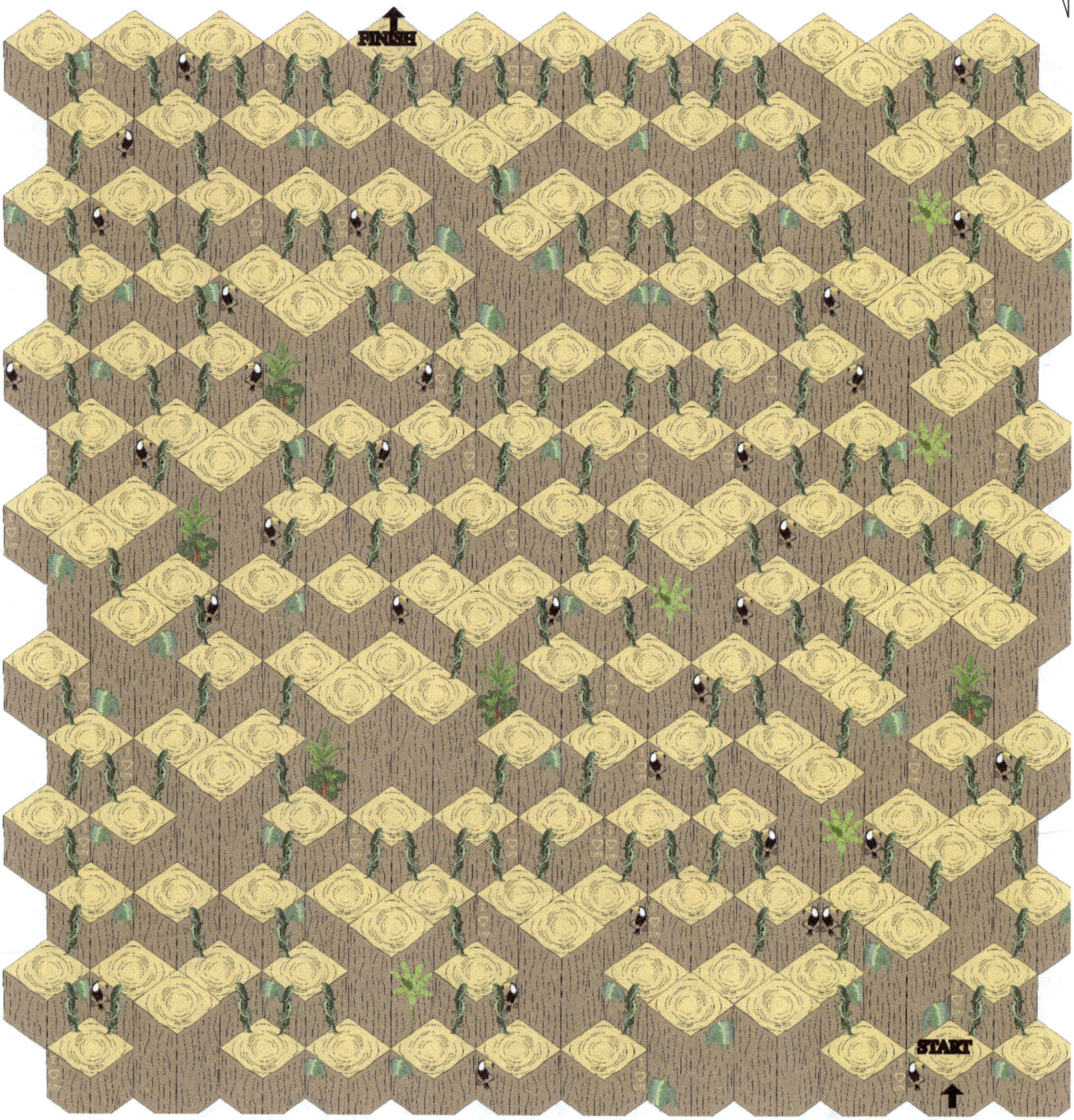

15

16

17

18

19

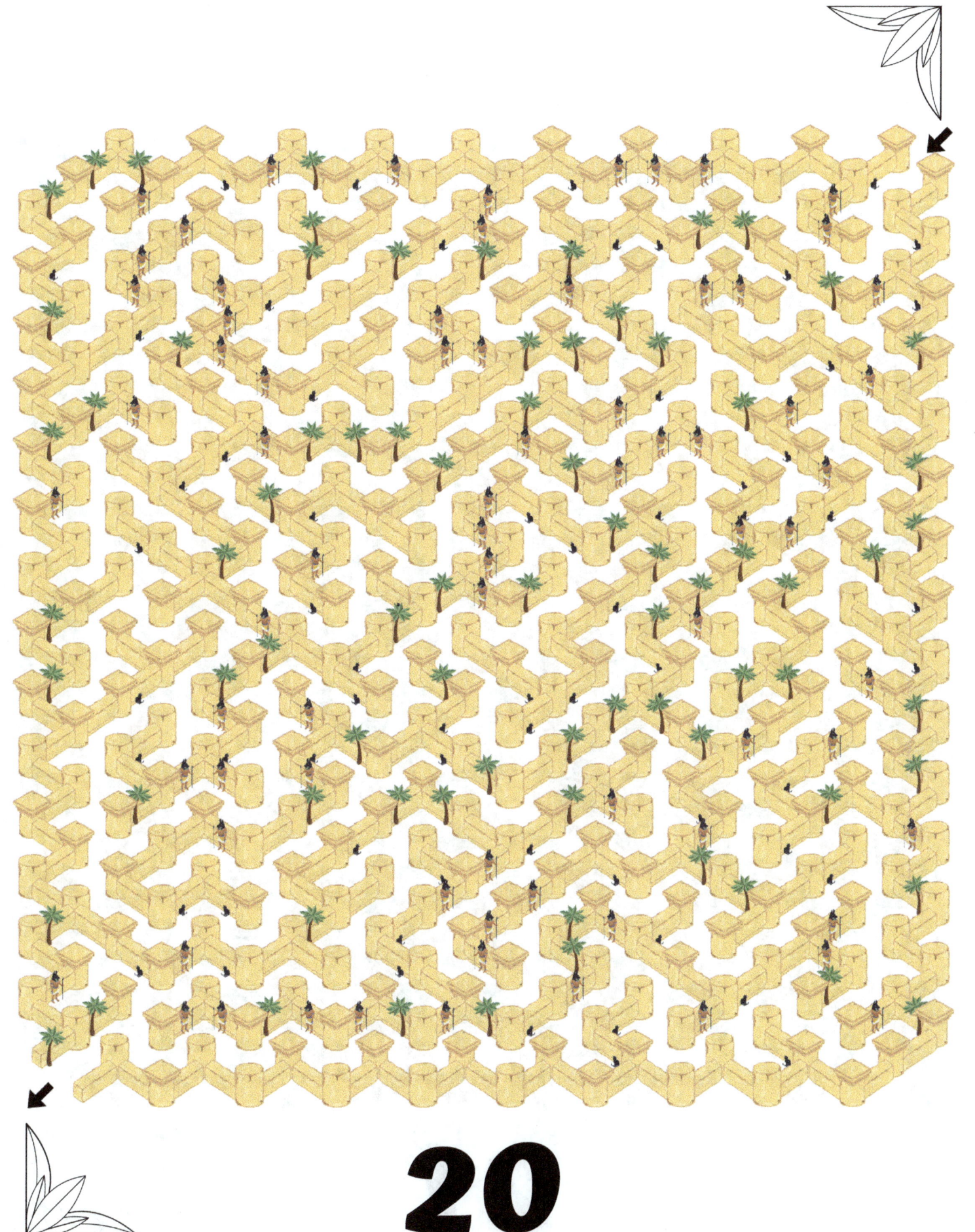

20

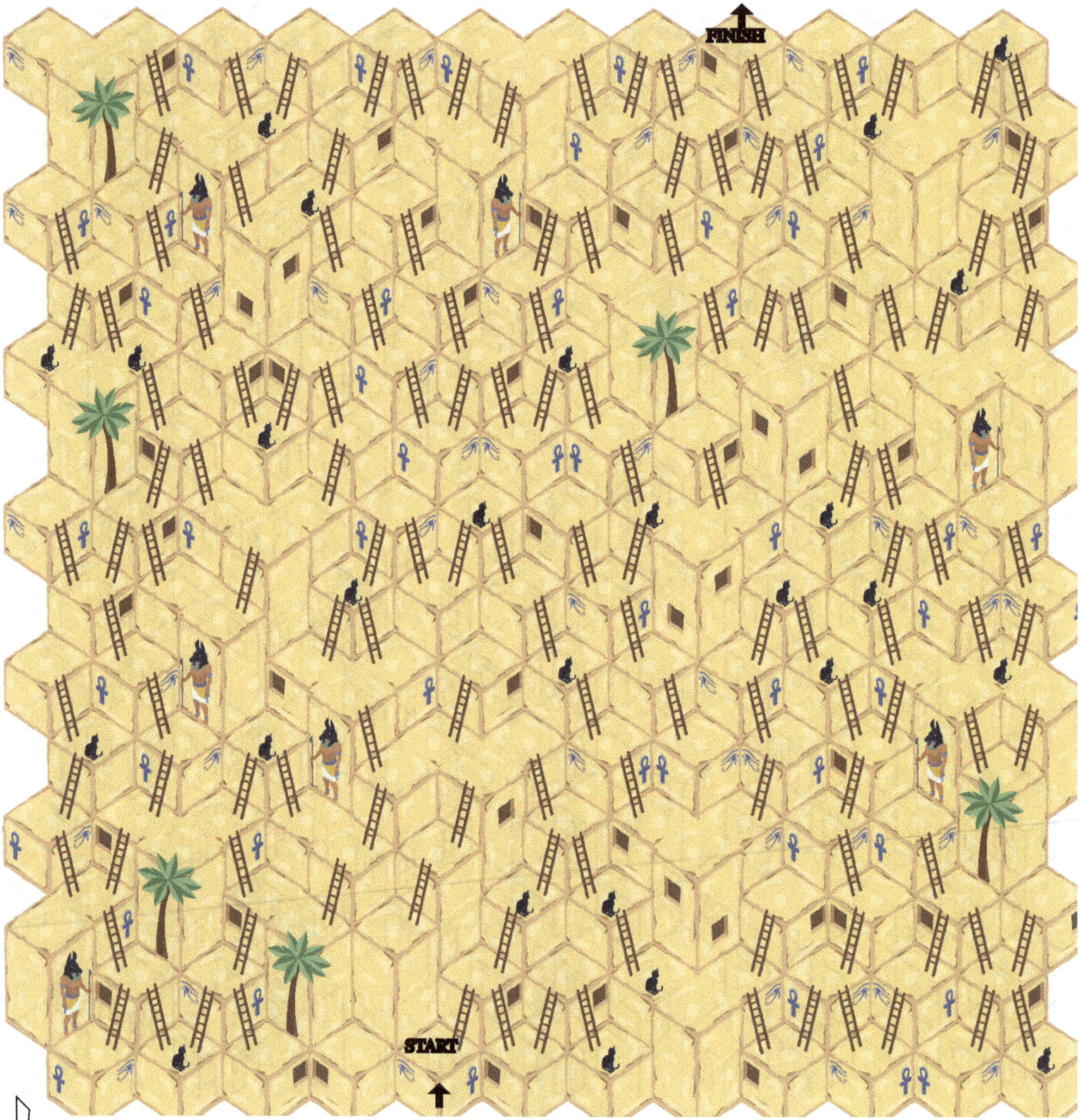

23

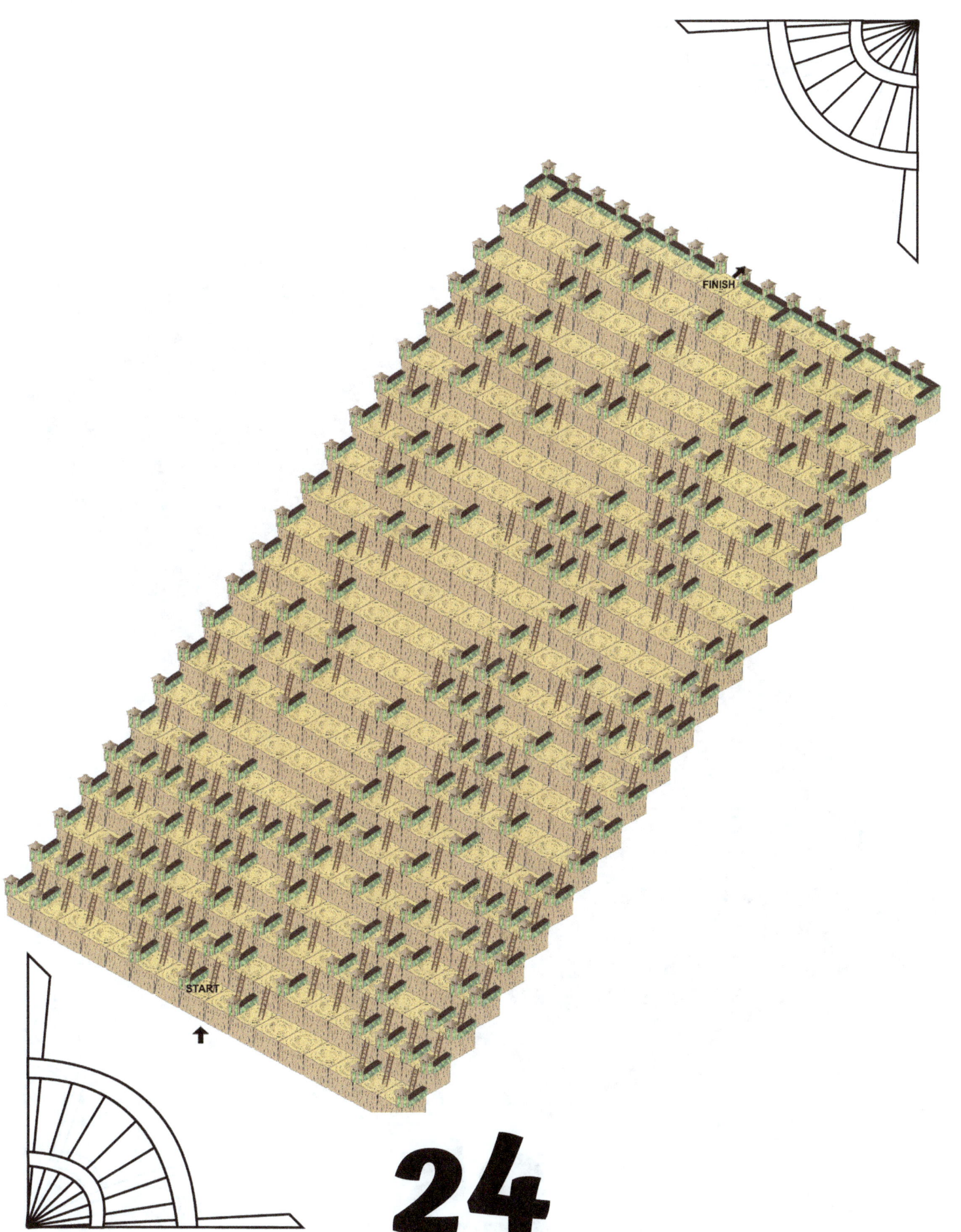

24

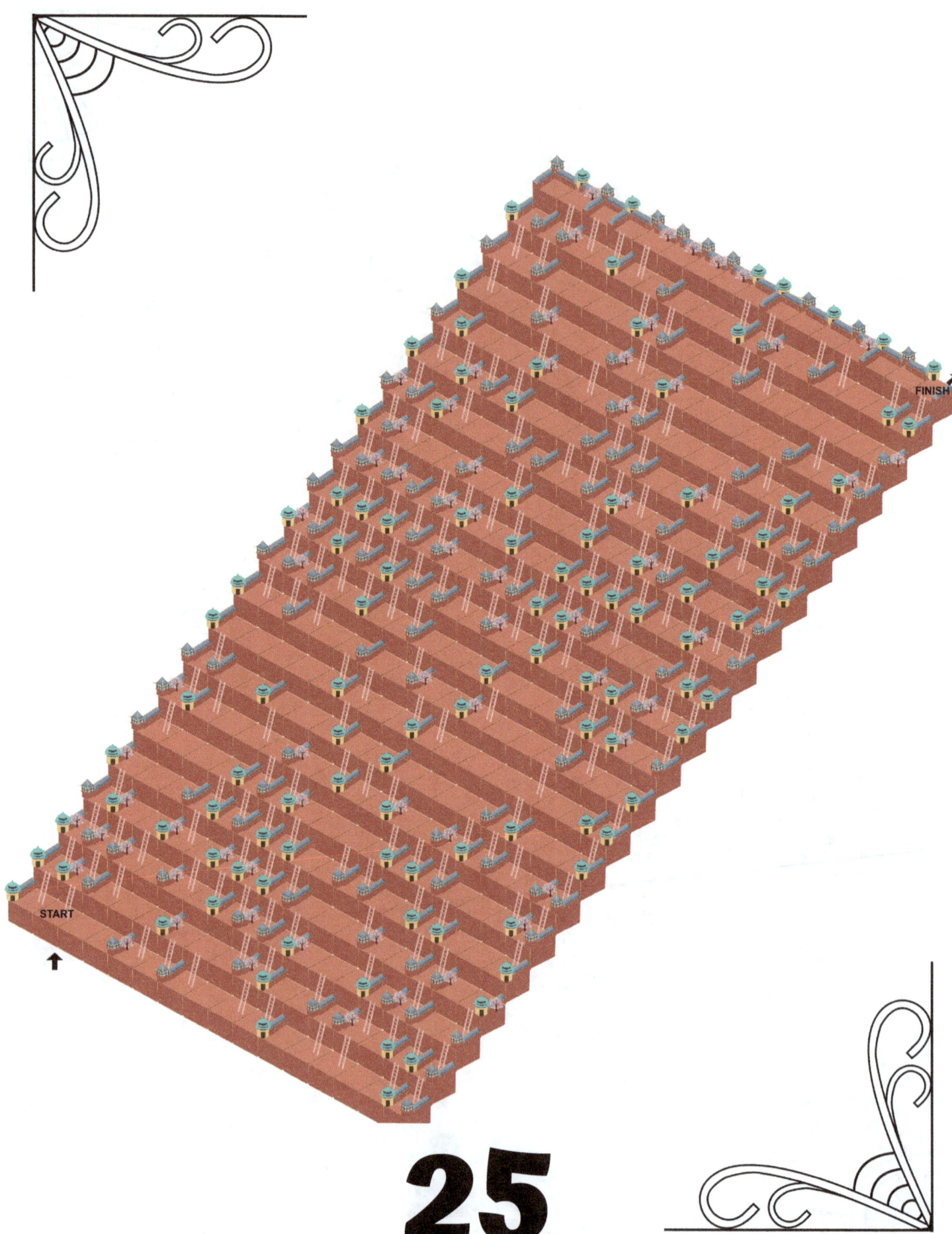

25

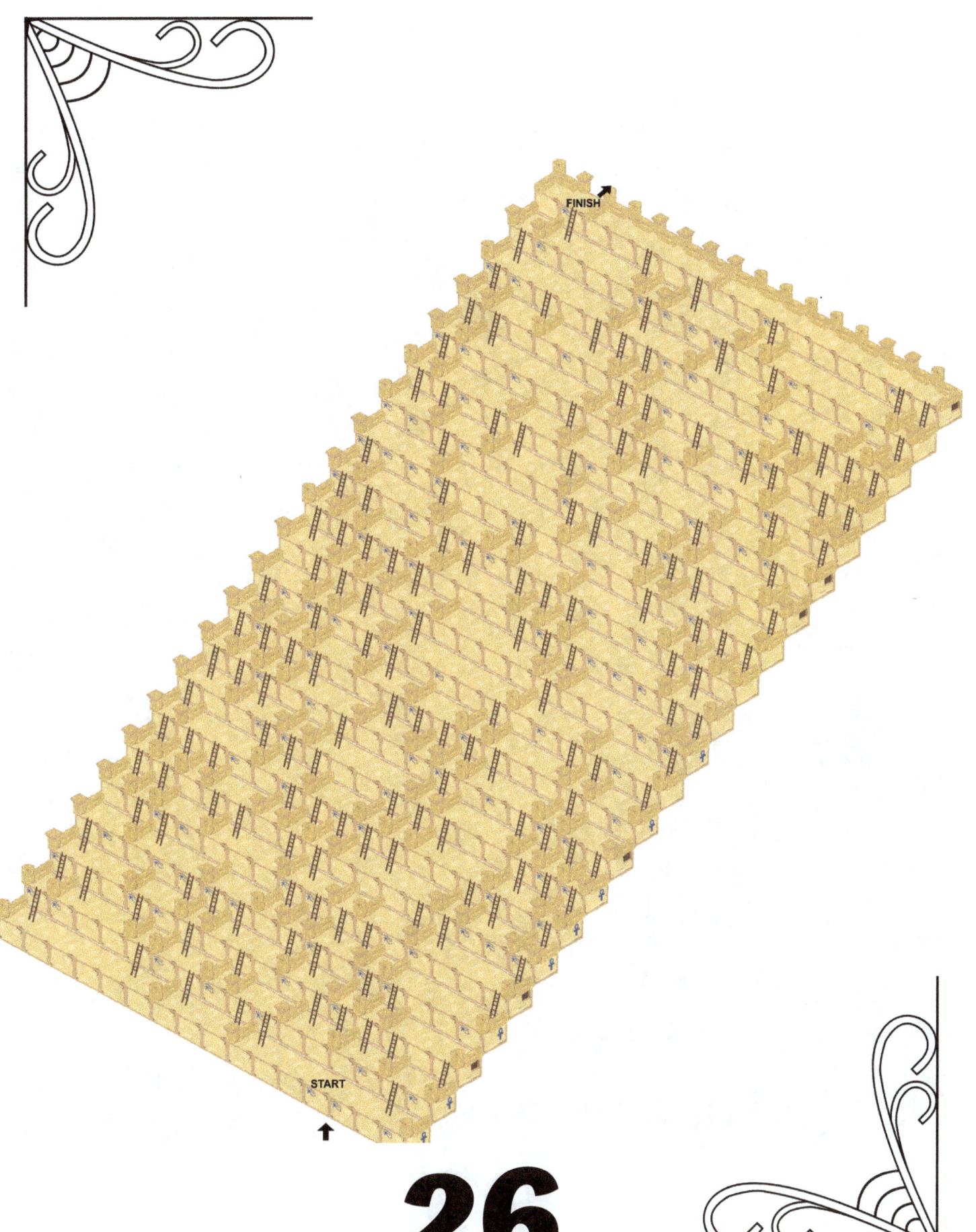

26

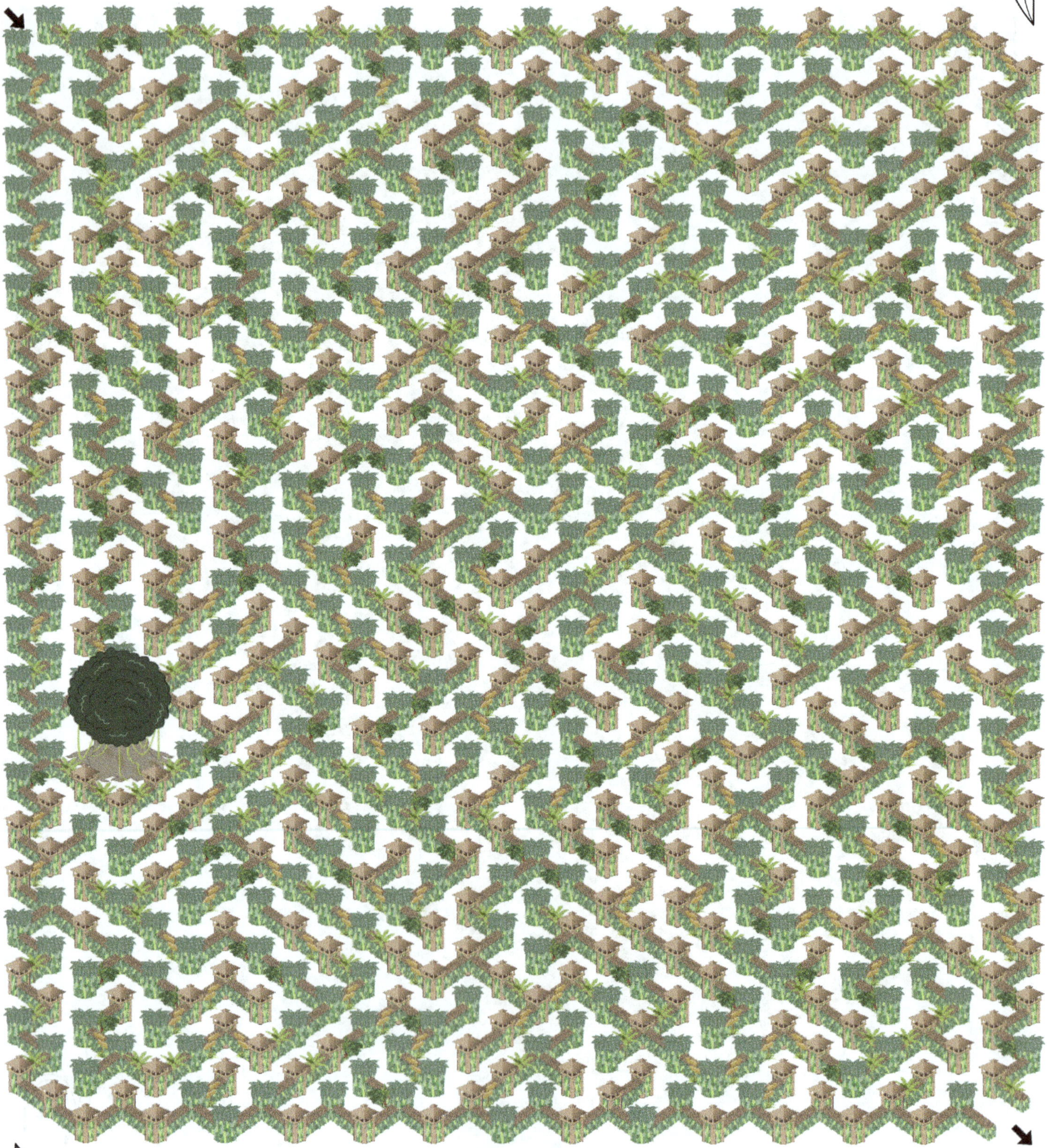

27

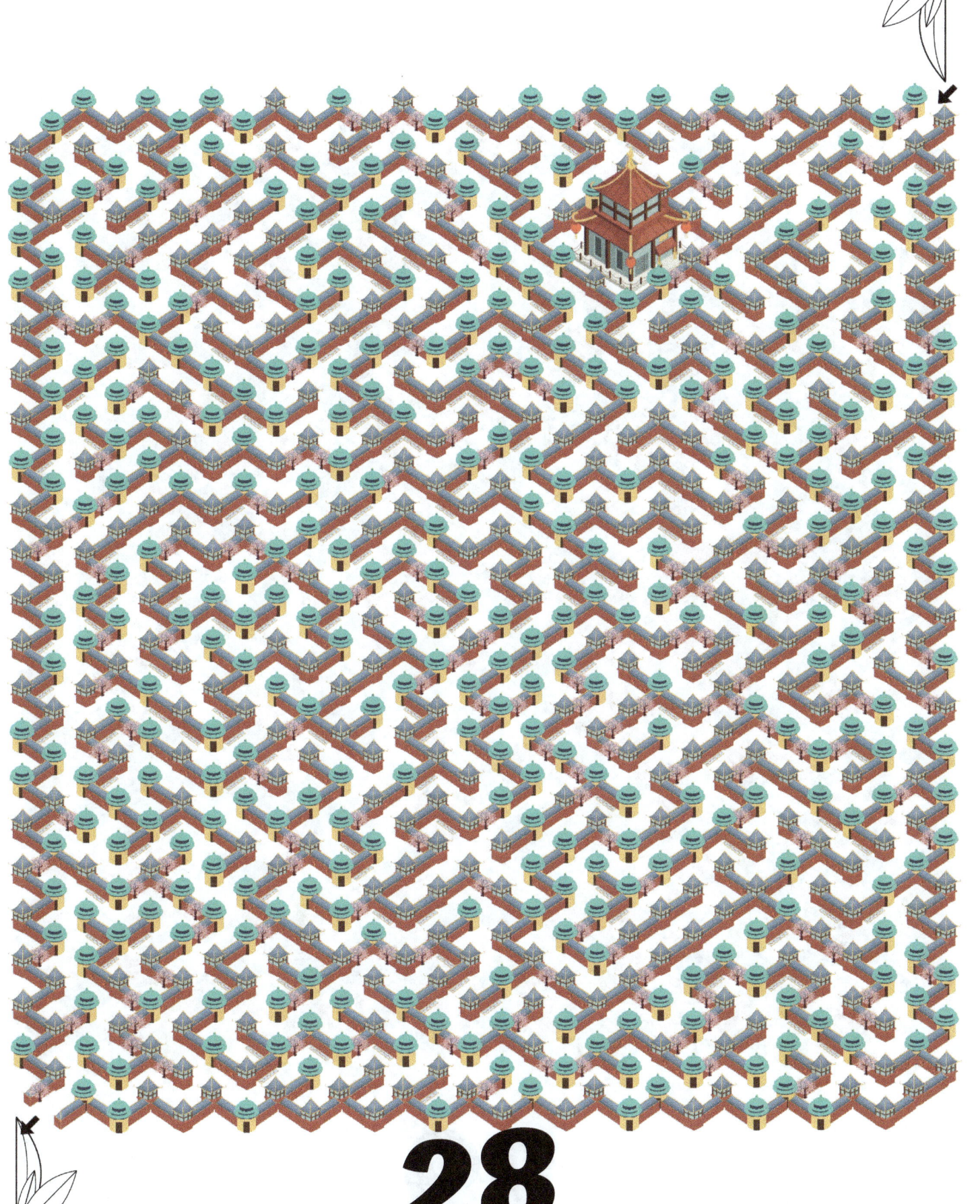

28

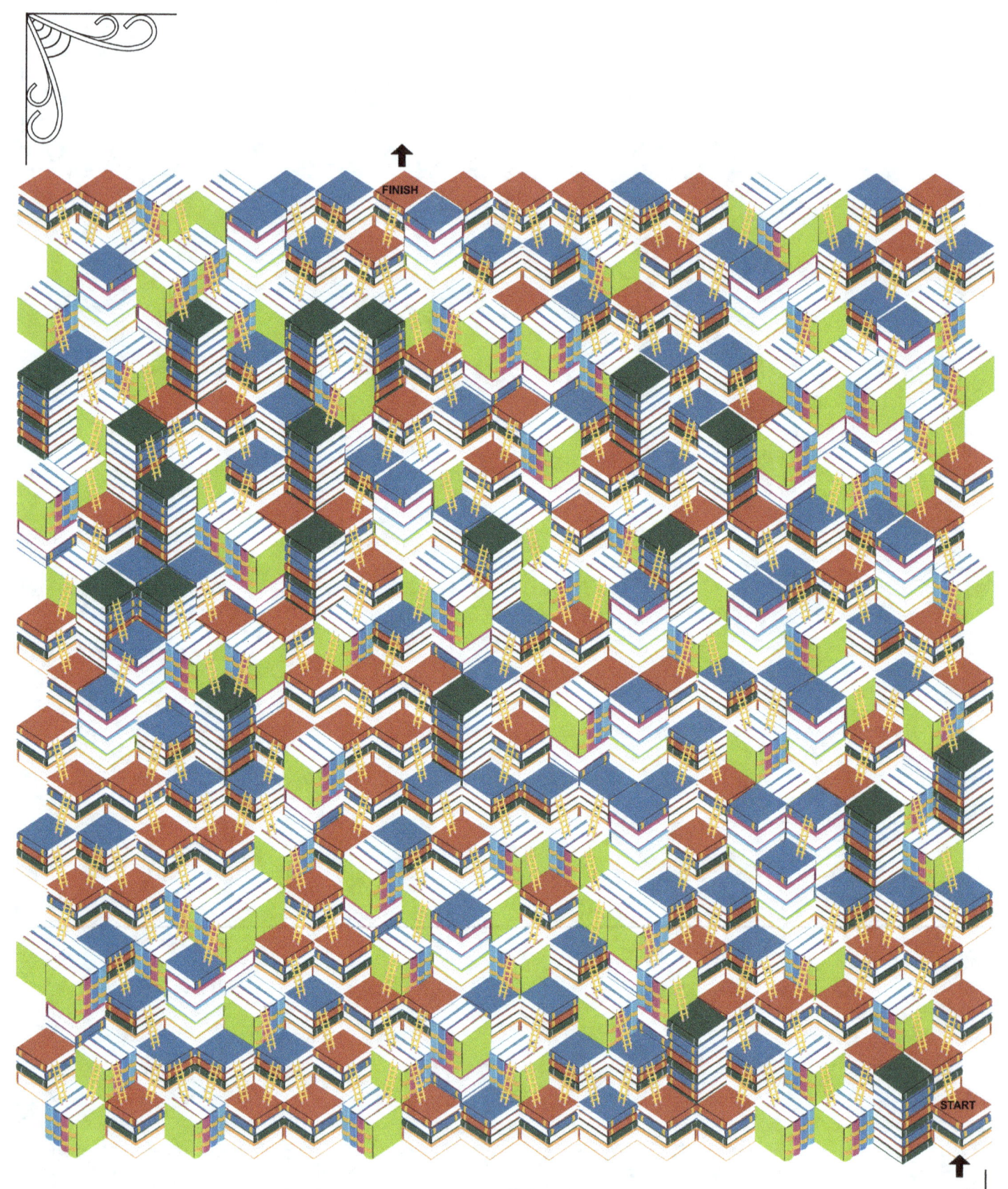

29

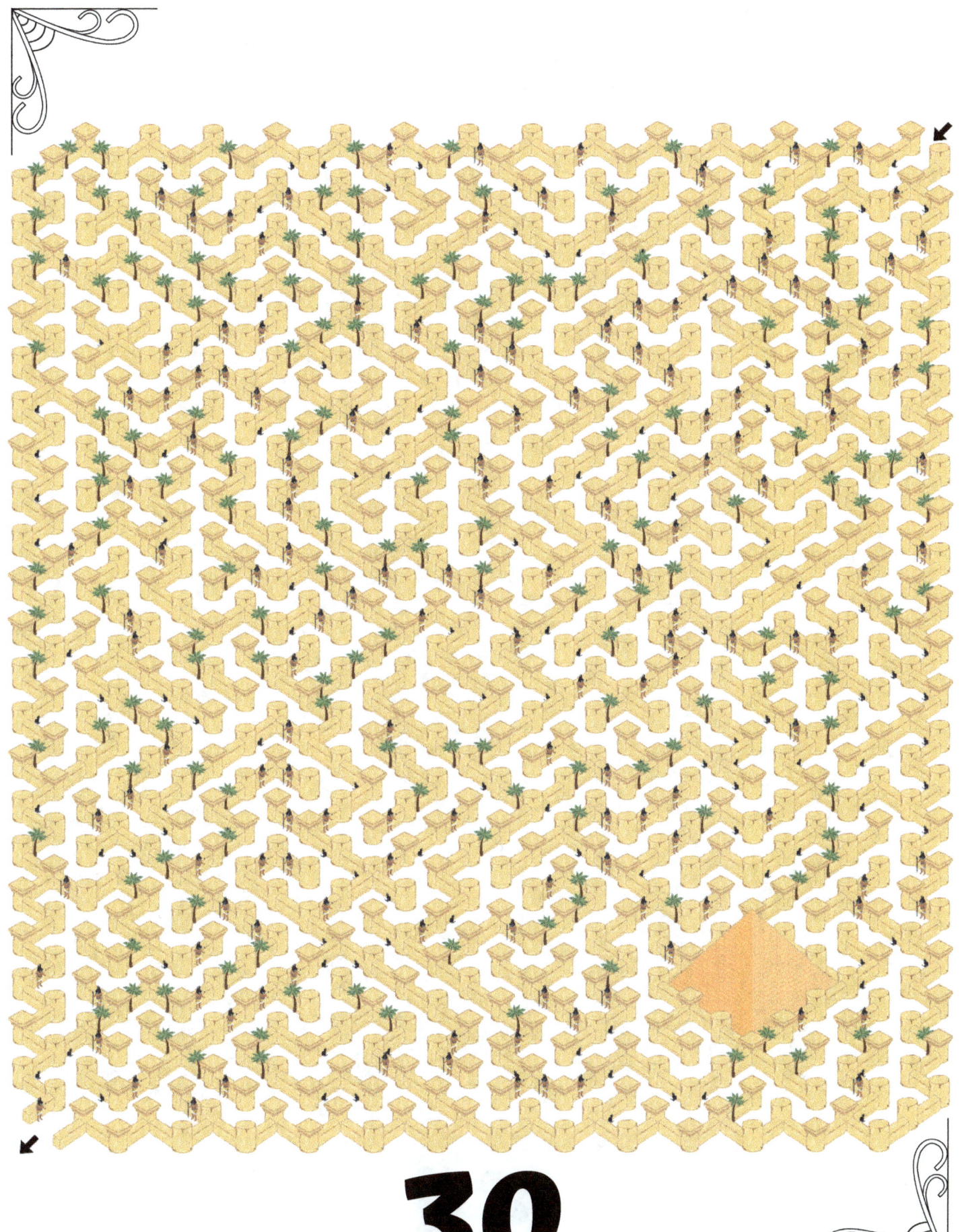

30

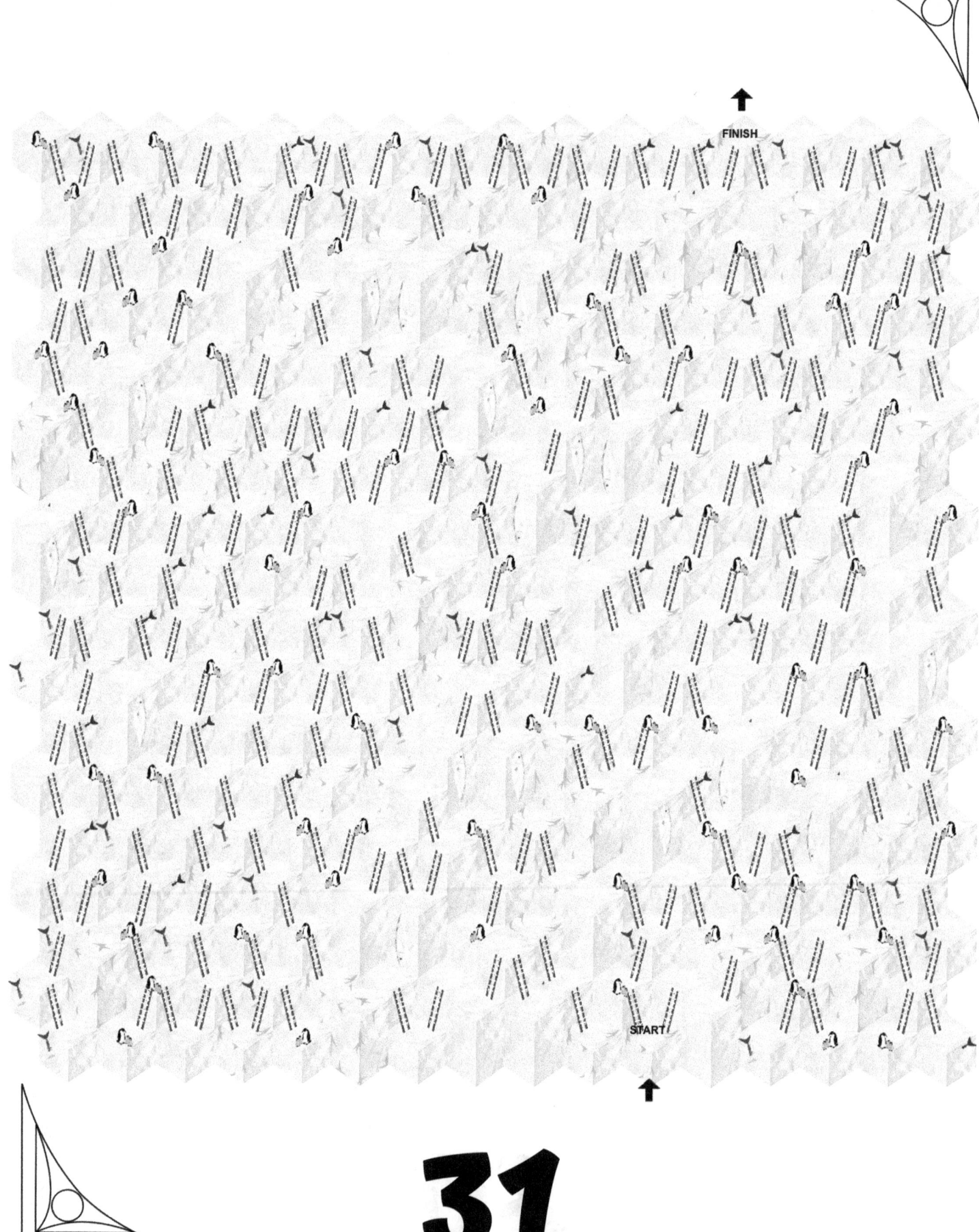

31

32

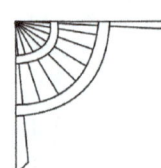

33

34

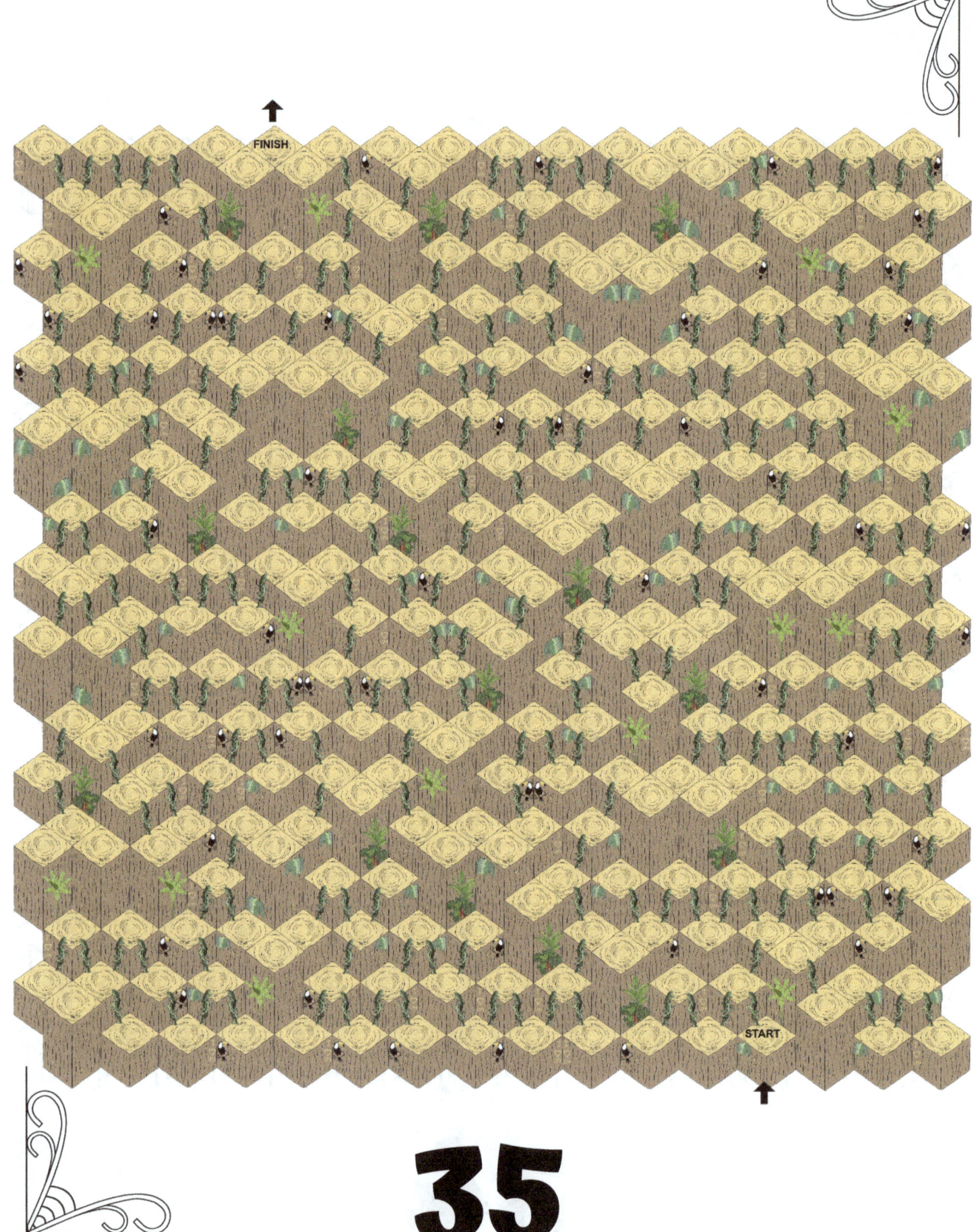

35

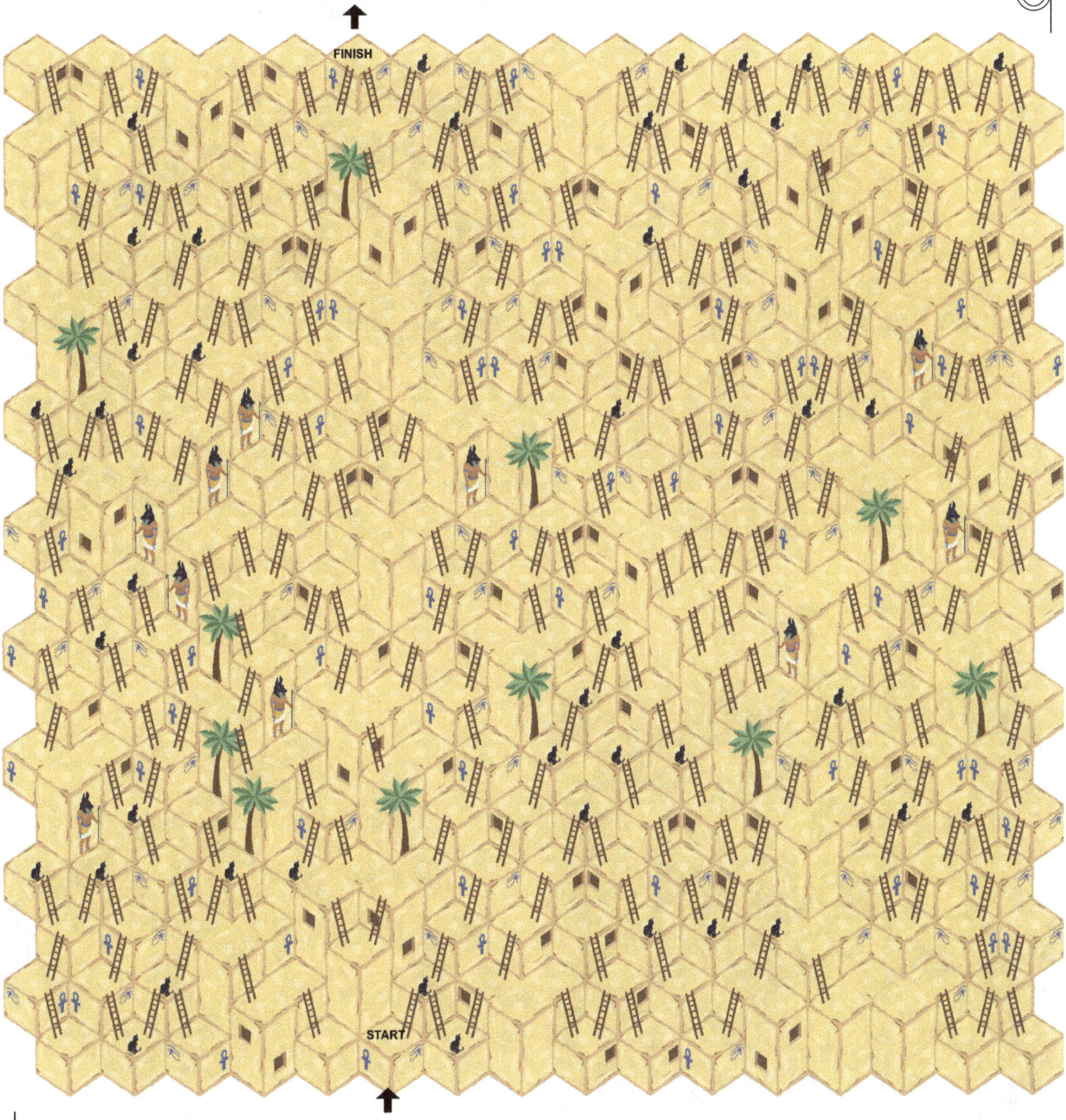

36

Solutions

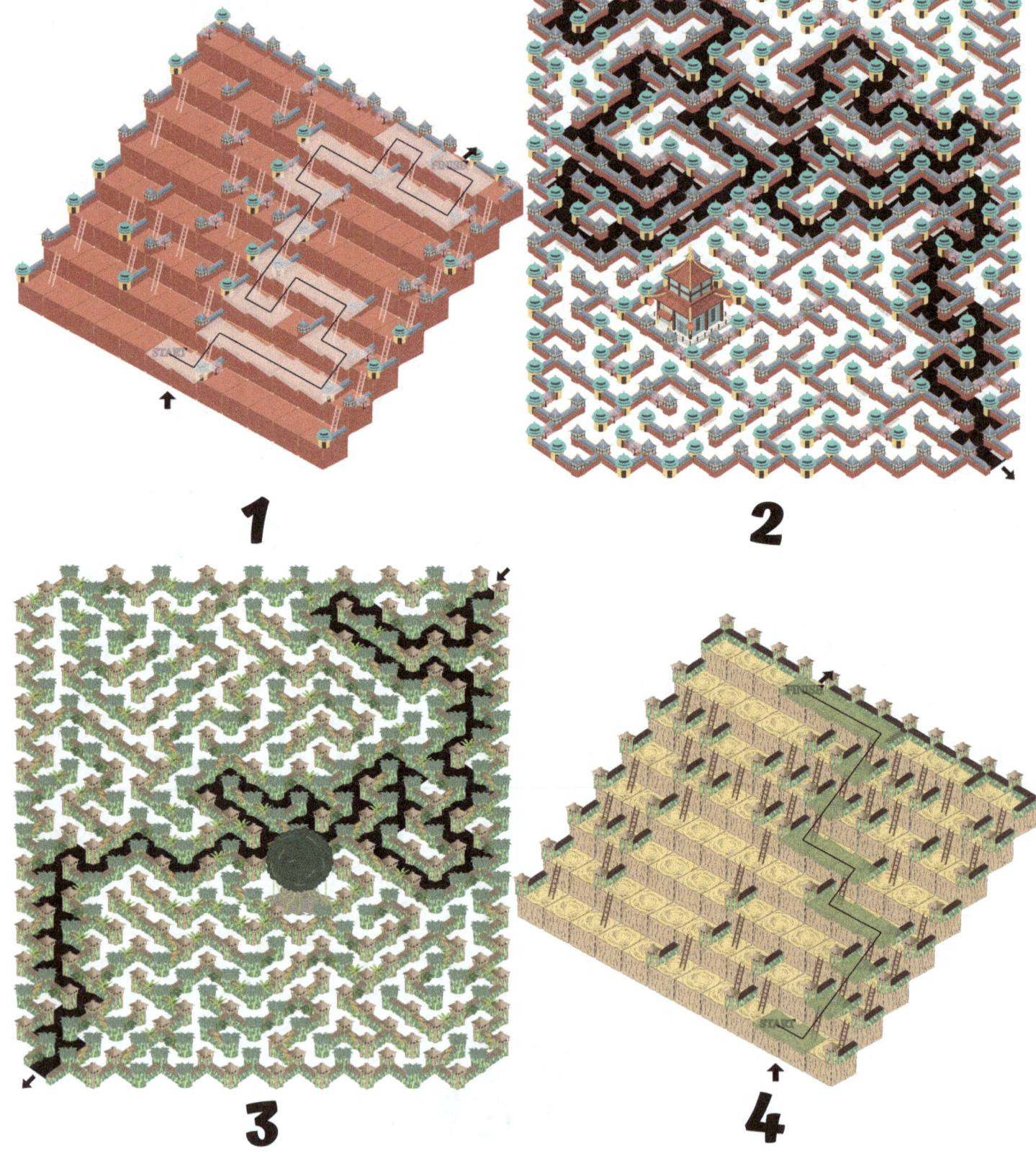

1

2

3

4

Solutions

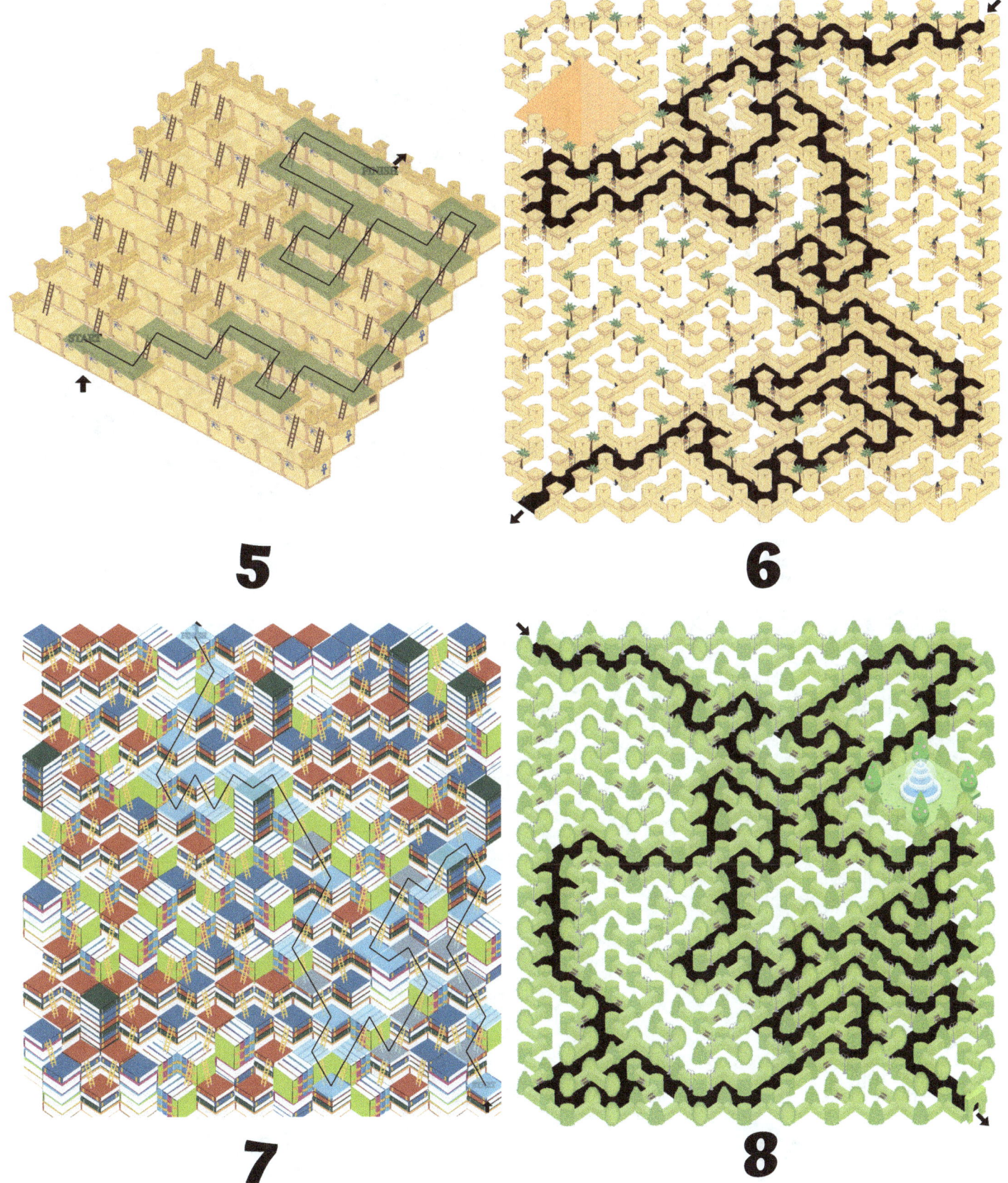

5

6

7

8

Solutions

9
10
11
12

Solutions

13

14

15

16

Solutions

17
18
19
20

Solutions

21

22

23

24

Solutions

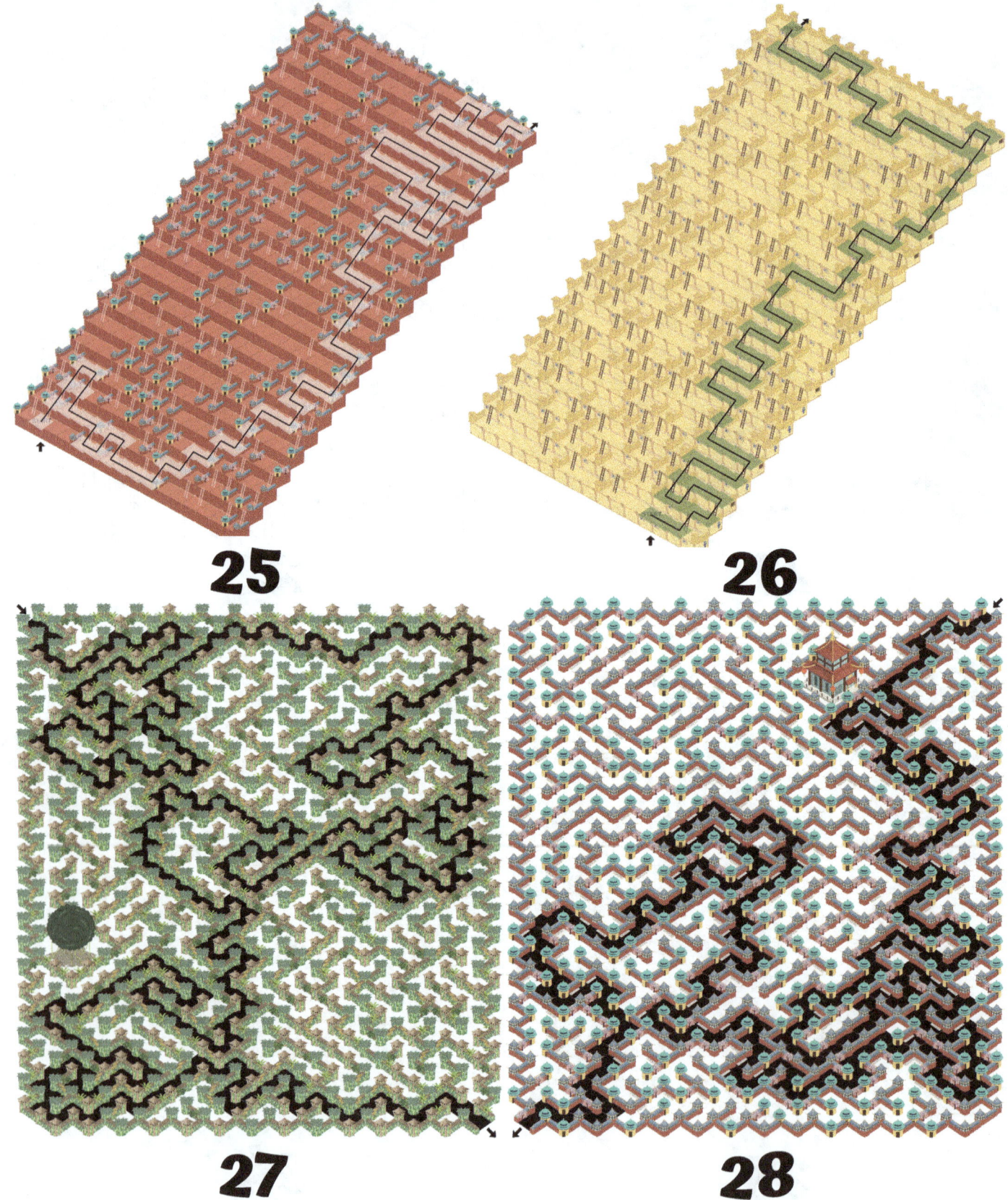

25
26
27
28

Solutions

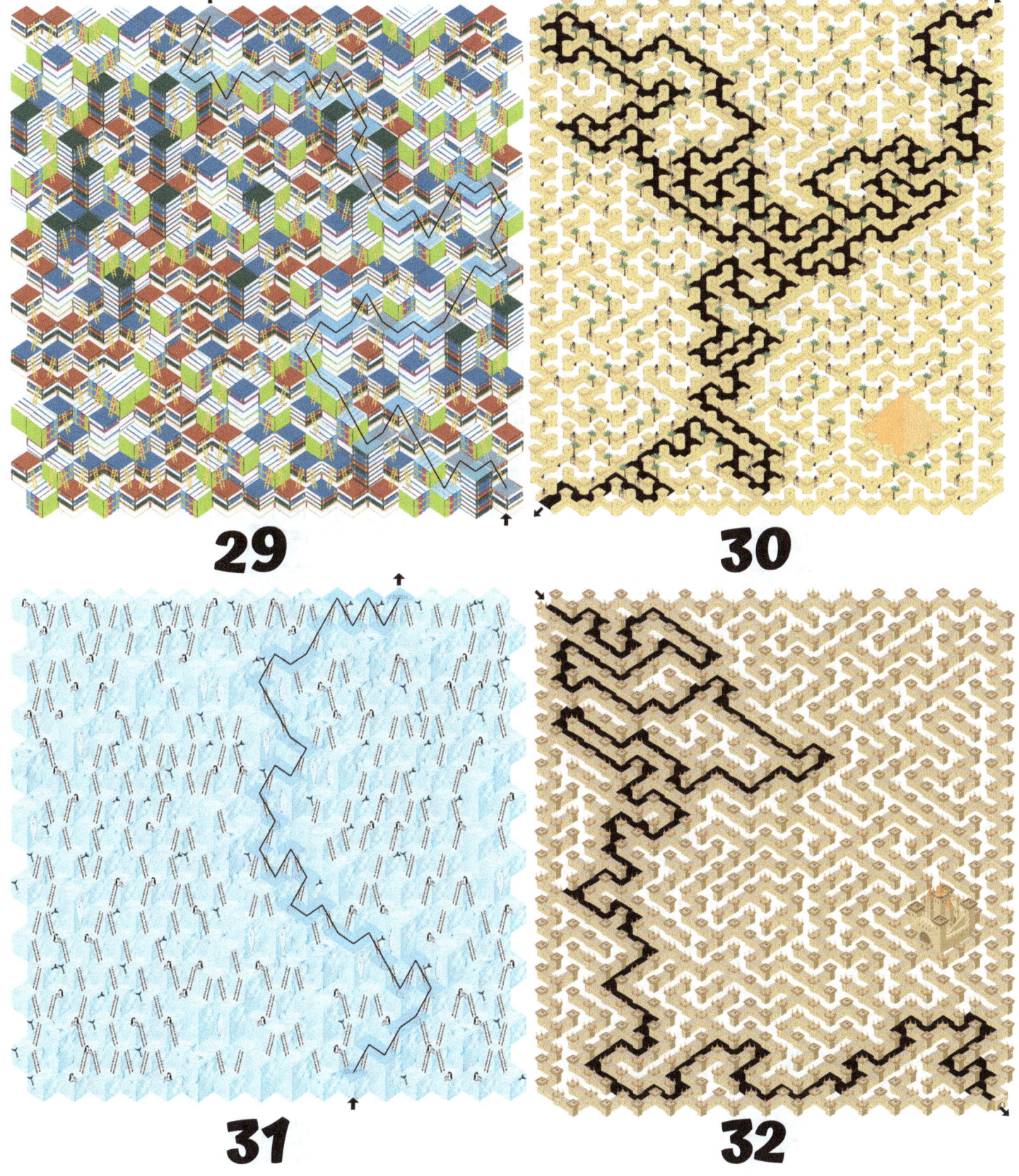

29

30

31

32

Solutions

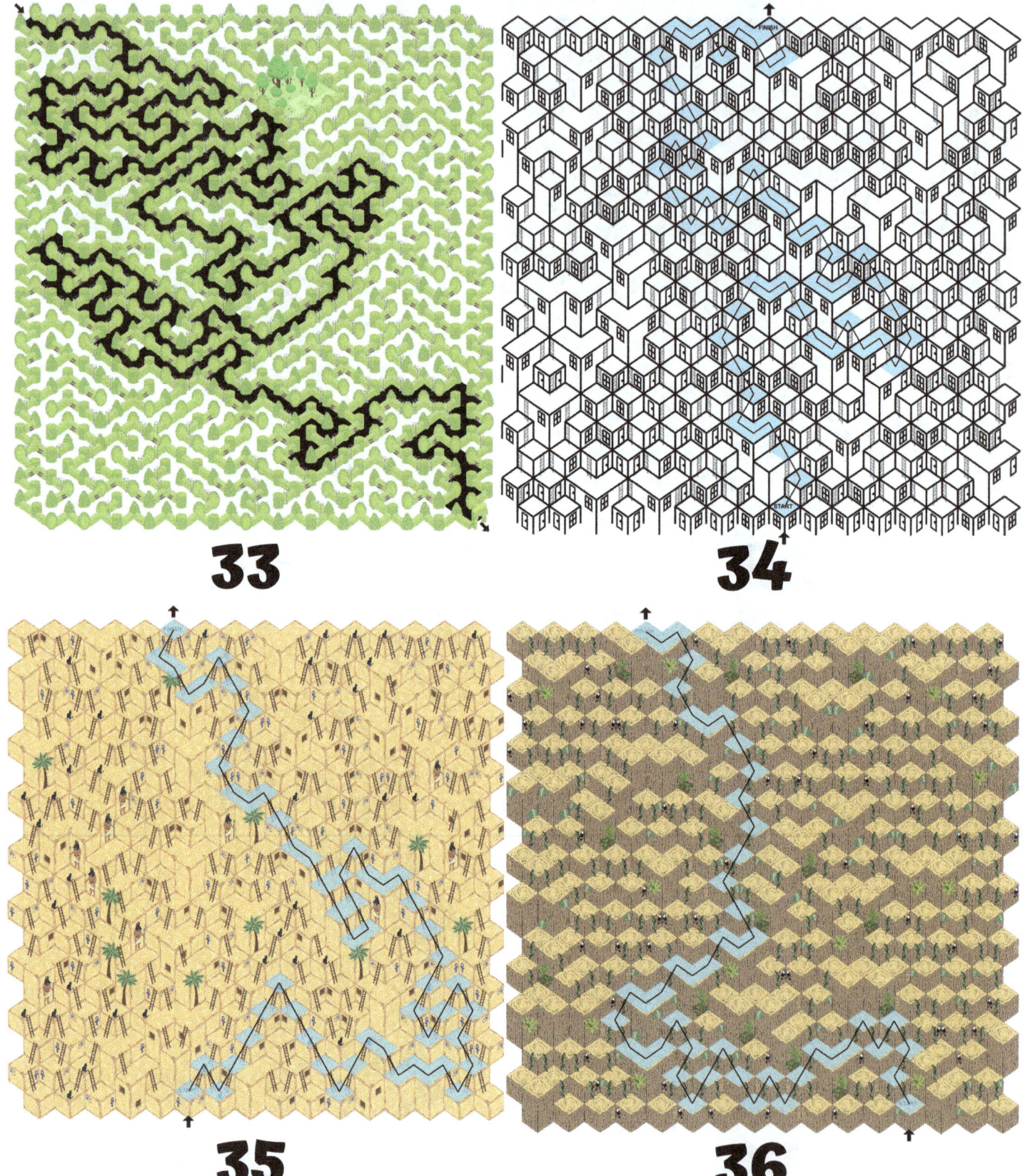

33
34
35
36

We hope you loved the mazes. If you did, would you consider posting an online review?

☆☆☆☆☆

This helps us to continue providing great products, and helps potential buyers to make confident decisions.

For more mazes, find our similar titles